Sunday

BIBLE

TRIVIA

200 Trivia questions designed to test your knowledge of the Bible, whether you are an believer or advanced in your faith.

Zach Windahl

INTRODUCTION

About Zach

My name is Zach Windahl and I created Sunday Bible Trivia because it is my goal in life to create tools for Christians to further their faith.

In 2014, I hit a low spot in my life. Like low low. Everything that I touched began to fail. I had never felt so lost. If you know me, you know I always have a plan. But this time I didn't. I was at the bottom. Broken and lost. I had spent the last several years focusing on myself and trying to become the best person I could be. But, to tell you the truth, I'm weak when I try to live life on my own. From the outside, everything looked great but the inside was a whole different story.

I started to contemplate what all of this was about. I grew up considering myself a Christian, but I had no idea what that truly meant. I hadn't been following God's call at all. I still believed in Him, I just wasn't pursuing Him. I hadn't been to church in over a year for the simple fact that I couldn't stand the majority of Christians that I met because I didn't trust them. They all seemed so fake. Little did I know that the darkness inside of me at the time didn't like the Light inside of them.

So I sat there thinking..."Is life really all about going to college, getting a job, getting married, having kids, buying new things, and then (hopefully) one day retiring so I can enjoy life?"

Really? That's it? That all seemed so shallow to me.

Then, let's look at religion. Every religion outside of Christianity takes their faith so seriously, it's insane. And then there's us. Where only 45% of Christians read the Bible once a month and the fact that a ton of "Christian" ideals are pretty skewed from the Bible itself. I was fed up. So I read the Bible. Front to back. In 90 days.
I was blown away by how different the Bible actually is, compared to how it's presented in America. But that's what makes us Christians, right? The fact that we believe and follow Jesus? Nothing was lining up. I was confused.

So I went on my own "Search for Meaning" journey. I quit my job and moved to a little beach town on the Sunshine Coast of Australia for 9-months to study the Bible for twelve hours per day. That's a pretty big leap if you ask me. And at 27 years old it may not have been the wisest of decisions, but I wouldn't have changed it for anything.

the Bible is good for you

My whole reason for this journey was to build a firm foundation in my faith - one that could not be crumbled by society. And that's exactly what I got, plus more.

And that's what my hope is for you. That you are able to build a firm foundation in your faith through tools like the Sunday Bible Trivia book. Especially in a time when understanding the Word is one of the most important things that you can do.

My God-sized dream is to help millions of people all over the world fall in love with the Word of God and actually understand what they were reading instead of being confused. In the Sunday Bible Trivia book, you will come across questions ranging from easy to hard. No matter if you know a lot, or know a little, my prayer is that you have a passion to dig deeper into the Word every day. If you want to learn more about the Bible, but aren't sure where to begin, our other product The Bible Study: A One Year Study of the Bible that focuses on How Each Book Relates to You is a great place to build your foundation.

If you would like to pick up your copy of The Bible Study today, please visit *www.thebrandsunday.com*.

DID YOU KNOW?

The Bible was originally written in 3 languages: Hebrew, Aramaic, and Greek.

It took over 1,000 years for the Old Testament to be written.

BIBLE TRIVIA

How it
WORKS

Sunday Bible Trivia

God is going to use these trivia questions to draw you closer to Him.

Sunday Bible Trivia is split into two main sections: *Old Testament and New Testament*

The questions are on one side, along with the answers and references on the reverse.

I couldn't be more excited for how God is going to use these trivia questions to draw you closer to Him. I love you. I believe in you.

Let's go!

-Z

Old Testament

Bible Trivia

100 questions and answers to test your knowledge of the Old Testament

Questions

1. What five books make up the Torah?

2. How many books are in the Old Testament?

3. What four types of literature are in the Old Testament?

4. What book describes creation?

5. What day did God create humanity?

6. Whose image were Adam and Eve made in?

7. What sin did Cain commit?

8. What was the name of Adam and Eve's son who was the "substitute" for Able?

9. What type of covenant did God make with Noah?

10. Who is referred to as the "Father of Faith"?

11. Who was Abraham asked to sacrifice?

the Bible is good for you

Answer Key

1. Genesis, Exodus, Leviticus, Numbers, Deuteronomy

2. 39

3. Historical, the Law, Wisdom, Poetry

4. Genesis (Genesis 1-2)

5. Day 6 (Genesis 1-2)

6. God's / "Our" image (Genesis 1:26)

7. Murder (Genesis 4:8)

8. Seth (Genesis 4:25)

9. A promissory covenant

10. Abraham

11. His son, Isaac (Genesis 22:2)

Questions

12. What were the names of Isaac's twins?

13. What did Jacob's name mean?

14. What was Esau doing while Jacob stole his blessing?

15. Who did Jacob wrestle with?

16. How many sons did Jacob have?

17. Which son of Jacob was sold into slavery?

18. What gift did God give to Joseph?

19. What caused Joseph's brothers to go to Egypt?

20. What did Jacob's 12 sons become?

21. How many years passed between Jacob's death and the book of Exodus?

22. Who wrote the book of Exodus?

23. What happened to the Israelites in Egypt during the 400 years after Jacob's death?

the Bible is good for you

Answer Key

12. Jacob and Esau (Genesis 25:25-26)

13. Deceiver (Genesis 25:26)

14. Hunting (Genesis 27:1-3)

15. God (Genesis 32:28)

16. 12 (Genesis 35:23-26)

17. Joseph (Genesis 37:36)

18. The ability to interpret dreams (Genesis 40:12)

19. A famine (Genesis 42:2)

20. The 12 tribes of Israel (Genesis 49:28)

21. 400

22. Moses

23. They were enslaved (Exodus 1:11)

Questions

24. What house did Moses grow up in?

25. What caused Moses to murder an Egyptian?

26. Where did Moses go after committing murder?

27. How long did Moses shepherd in the wilderness for?

28. How did God appear to Moses while he was in the wilderness?

29. When God appeared to Moses through the burning bush, what did He say about the ground that Moses was standing on?

30. What did God instruct for Moses to tell Pharaoh?

31. How many plagues came upon Egypt for their disobedience?

32. What did God use each plague to mock?

33. What happened to Pharaoh's heart after he refused God's instructions?

the Bible is good for you

Answer Key

24. Pharaoh's house (Exodus 2:10)

25. The Egyptian was abusing a Hebrew (Exodus 2:11)

26. Midian (Exodus 2:15)

27. 40 years (Exodus 2)

28. Through a burning bush (Exodus 3:2)

29. It was Holy ground (Exodus 3:5)

30. To let His people (the Israelites) go from slavery (Exodus 3:10)

31. 10 (Exodus 7-11)

32. The false gods of the Egyptians

33. God hardened his heart (Exodus 9:12)

Questions

34. Which plague finally caused Pharaoh to let the Israelites go from slavery?

35. Which sea did God use Moses to part after fleeing Egypt?

36. What did God provide for the Israelites to eat in the wilderness?

37. How many commandments did God give the Israelites on Mount Sinai?

38. Where was God's glory found during the years that the Israelites roamed the desert?

39. In Leviticus, how many "rules" or regulations did God give the Israelites?

40. Why did God tell the Israelites to live Holy lives?

41. Which of the two spies sent by Moses and Aaron to scout out the Promised Land are known for their faith?

the Bible is good for you

Answer Key

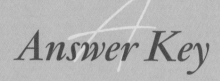

34. Death of the firstborn son (Exodus 11-12)

35. The Red Sea

36. Manna aka bread from Heaven (Exodus 16:4)

37. 10 (Exodus 20)

38. The Tabernacle (Exodus 40:34)

39. 613

40. Because He is holy (Leviticus 19:2)

41. Joshua and Caleb

Questions

42. What animal did Moses compare the people of Israel to?

43. Why wasn't Moses allowed to enter the Promised Land?

44. Which book of the Bible deals with the death of Moses?

45. Who was the leader of the Israelites after Moses died?

46. Who hid the Israelite spies in Jericho?

47. Whose feet had to touch the Jordan River for the water to part?

48. How many stones did Joshua set up as an act of remembrance after crossing the Jordan?

49. On the seventh day of marching around the wall of Jericho, what instrument had to be blown for the walls to come down?

the Bible is good for you

Answer Key

42. Sheep (Numbers 27:17)

43. Because he disobeyed God / struck the rock instead of speaking to it (Deuteronomy 32:51-52)

44. Deuteronomy (Deuteronomy 34:5)

45. Joshua (Joshua 1:5)

46. Rahab (Joshua 2:3-4)

47. The priest's feet (Joshua 3:13)

48. 12 (Joshua 4:9)

49. A trumpet (Joshua 6:16)

Questions

50. Who said, "As for me and my house, we will serve the Lord"?

51. How many people were with Gideon in his victory over the Midianites?

52. Which of the judges in the Old Testament tore a lion apart with his bare hands?

53. What was the source of Samson's strength?

54. Who said, "Your people will be my people, and your God, my God"?

55. Who was considered the Kinsman Redeemer?

56. What was the name of Ruth's great-grandson?

57. Who was the first king that God chose for the Israelites?

58. How did God describe David?

59. Why did God's anointing leave Saul?

Answer Key

50. Joshua (Joshua 24:15)

51. 300 (Judges 7:8)

52. Samson (Judges 14:6)

53. His hair (Judges 16:17)

54. Ruth (Ruth 1:16)

55. Boaz (Ruth 3:9)

56. King David (Ruth 4:22)

57. Saul (1 Samuel 9:17)

58. A man after His own heart (1 Samuel 13:14)

59. He refused to obey God (1 Samuel 15:11)

Questions

60. Which of Jesse's sons was anointed to replace Saul?

61. In David's defeat of Goliath, how many stones did he pick up before the fight?

62. Who killed themselves so David would become the king over Judah?

63. How old was David when he became King?

64. Who became king after David and is known as the wisest man to ever live?

65. How many years did it take for Solomon to build his own house?

66. What did Elisha ask Elijah to give him before God took Elijah up in a whirlwind?

67. Which king started building God's temple?

68. Which king was 7 years old when he started to rule?

69. Who were the good kings of Israel and Judah?

the Bible is good for you

Answer Key

60. David (1 Samuel 16:13)

61. 5 (1 Samuel 17:40)

62. Saul (2 Samuel 1)

63. 30 (2 Samuel 5:4)

64. King Solomon (1 Kings 1:30)

65. 13 years (1 Kings 7:1)

66. A double portion of Elijah's blessing (2 Kings 2:9)

67. Solomon (2 Chronicles 3:1)

68. Joash (2 Chronicles 24:1)

69. Asa, Jehoshaphat, Hezekiah, Josiah (1-2 Chronicles)

Questions

70. Which king wrote a letter to Ezra?

71. What was Nehemiah's job for King Artaxerxes?

72. How many feasts did Queen Esther throw the king before making her special request?

73. What was one thing God did not allow Satan to take from Job?

74. Who were most of the Psalms written by?

75. Which Old Testament book is known as a collection of song lyrics?

76. What type for literature is the book of Proverbs considered to be?

77. What does the book of Ecclesiastes say about material things?

78. Which Old Testament book teaches about a holy marriage and healthy romantic relationships?

the Bible is good for you

Answer Key

70. King Artaxerxes (Ezra 7:11)

71. He was the cup-bearer (Nehemiah 2:1)

72. 2 (Esther)

73. His life (Job 1:12)

74 David

75. Psalms

76. Wisdom Literature

77. They are meaningless (Ecclesiastes 1:2)

78. Song of Songs

Questions

79. What year was the Kingdom of Israel divided into the Northern and Southern Kingdoms?

80. What World Power did the Northern Kingdom fall to in 722 B.C.?

81. Who was the king of Babylon when they destroyed the Southern Kingdom of Judah in 586 B.C.?

82. Which prophet is known as the "weeping prophet"?

83. How many years was Israel in Babylon?

84. Who did God instruct to prophesy to dry bones?

85. Which Old Testament figure was known as both a prophet AND a priest?

86. Which book is known as the "Revelation of the Old Testament"?

87. How was Daniel protected in the lion's den?

the Bible is good for you

Answer Key

79. 930 B.C.

80. Assyria (2 Kings 17:3-23)

81. King Nebuchadnezzar (2 Chronicles 36:15-21)

82. Jeremiah (Jeremiah 4:19)

83. 70 (Jeremiah 29:10)

84. Ezekiel (Ezekiel 37:4)

85. Ezekiel

86. Book of Daniel

87. An angel shut the mouths of the lions (Daniel 6:22)

Questions

88. What three men were thrown into a furnace because of their faith and came out unburned?

89. Which gentile king built a golden statue of himself?

90. What did Daniel interpret for King Belshazzar?

91. Which four prophets in the Old Testament are considered the "Major Prophets"?

92. Which twelve books in the Old Testament are considered the "Minor Prophets"?

93. Which prophet was believed to be a disciple of Isaiah?

94. What type of woman did God tell the prophet Hosea to marry?

95. In the final chapter of Joel, how long did God say Judah would be inhabited?

96. Which Old Testament book is the shortest?

the Bible is good for you

Answer Key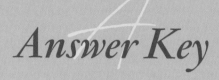

88. Shadrach, Meshach, and Abednego (Daniel 3:23-27)

89. King Nebuchadnezzar (Daniel 3)

90. The handwriting on the wall (Daniel 5)

91. Isaiah, Jeremiah, Ezekiel, and Daniel

92. Hosea, Joel, Amos, Obadiah, Jonah, Micah, Nahum, Habakkuk, Zephaniah, Haggai, Zechariah, and Malachi

93. Micah

94. A prostitute (Hosea 1:2)

95. Forever (Joel 3:20)

96. Obadiah

Questions

97. Which prophet was swallowed by a fish before sharing God's message of forgiveness to the city of Nineveh?

98. Who did God say He would make His signet ring?

99. Which prophet's name also means "My Messenger"?

100. How much time passed between the Old and New Testaments?

the Bible is good for you

Answer Key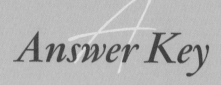

97.   Jonah (Jonah 1:17)

98.   Zerubbabel (Haggai 2:23)

99.   Malachi

100. 400 years

DID YOU KNOW?

Everyone on Earth spoke the same language until the Tower of Babel.

Ruth's great grandson was King David.

DID YOU KNOW?

God's title "Jehovah Jireh" means "He will provide".

Jesus and John the Baptist were actually cousins.

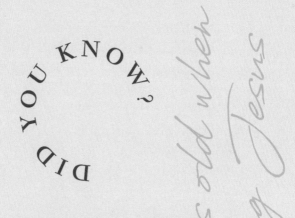

DID YOU KNOW?

Jesus had at least six half siblings.

The apostle John was believed to be 14 years old when he first started following Jesus.

New Testament

Bible Trivia

100 questions and answers to test your knowledge of the New Testament

Questions

1.   What does the word "gospel" mean?

2.   Which books make up the four gospels?

3.   Who was Matthew writing to in the Gospel of Matthew?

4.   Who were the parents of Jesus?

5.   What town was Jesus born in?

6.   When Jesus was a baby, who wanted to kill him?

7.   Who was the mother of John the Baptist?

8.   Where did Jesus go when his parents lost him?

9.   What did John the Baptist say when he saw Jesus?

10. During Jesus' baptism, what form did the Holy Spirit take?

11. What age did Jesus start his ministry?

the Bible is good for you

Answer Key

1. Good news

2. Matthew, Mark, Luke and John

3. The Jews

4. Mary and Joseph (Luke 2:1-8)

5. Bethlehem (Matthew 2:1)

6. Herod the Great (Matthew 2:13)

7. Elizabeth (Luke 1:13)

8. The temple (Luke 2:41-52)

9. "Behold, the lamb of God!" (John 1:29)

10. A dove (Luke 3:22)

11. 30 (Luke 3:23)

Questions

12. How long was Jesus in the wilderness where he was tempted by Satan?

13. What was the first temptation of Jesus?

14. What was the purpose of Jesus coming to Earth?

15. What does the word "Gentile" mean?

16. What does the word "Rabbi" mean?

17. What is a disciple?

18. What words does Jesus use when recruiting his disciples?

19. What was Jesus' first miracle?

20. Which disciple called himself, "the one who Jesus loves"?

21. What nationality was the woman at the well?

22. Which disciple tried to walk on water with Jesus?

the Bible is good for you

Answer Key

12. 40 days (Matthew 4:2)

13. To turn a stone into bread (Matthew 4:3)

14. To seek and save the lost (Luke 19:10)

15. Anyone who was non-Jewish

16. Teacher

17. A student or apprentice

18. "Follow me" (Matthew 9:9; Mark 1:17; Luke 5:27; John 1:43)

19. Turning water into wine (John 2:9)

20. John (John 13:23)

21. Samaritan (John 4:7)

22. Simon Peter (Matthew 14:29)

Questions

23. Which disciple was a tax collector before following Jesus?

24. What was the name of the man who asked Jesus to heal his daughter who was dying?

25. Why type of servant is Jesus referred to in Mark?

26. What did Jesus use to feed the 5,000?

27. After Jesus healed the blind man in Bethsaida, what did Jesus tell him not to do?

28. If you want to follow Jesus, you must pick up your what?

29. What type of tree did Jesus curse?

30. Jesus said that it is easier for a camel to go through the eye of a needle than a rich man to, what?

31. Why shouldn't we give anyone the title "Father"?

32. Which two prophets showed up at the Mount of Transfiguration with Jesus?

the Bible is good for you

Answer Key

23. Matthew (Matthew 9:9)

24. Jairus (Mark 5:22)

25. Suffering servant (Mark 8:31)

26. 5 loaves and 2 fish (Mark 6:38)

27. Do not go into the city (Mark 8:26)

28. Crosses (Mark 8:34)

29. A fig tree (Mark 11:14)

30. To enter the kingdom of God (Mark 10:25)

31. We have one Father who is in heaven (Matthew 23:9)

32. Elijah and Moses (Matthew 17:3)

Questions

33. How many pieces of silver did Judas receive for betraying Jesus?

34. The Gospel of John focuses on Jesus being fully God and fully, what?

35. What three parts make up the trinity?

36. Which gospel talks about the Holy Spirit the most?

37. What is the shortest verse in the Bible?

38. After Lazarus died, what did Jesus say at the entrance of his tomb?

39. How many "I am" statements are in the Gospel of John?

40. What are all of Jesus' "I am" statements in the Gospel of John?

41. How are we able to get to know God the Father?

42. What animal does Jesus ride into Jerusalem on?

the Bible is good for you

Answer Key

33. 30 (Matthew 26:15)

34. Human/Man

35. God the Father, God the Son, and God the Holy Spirit

36. Luke

37. "Jesus wept" (John 11:35)

38. "Lazarus, come out!" (John 11:43)

39. 7 (John 6:35; 8:12; 10:9; 10:11; 11:25; 14:6; 15:5)

40. I am the bread of life (John 6:35), the light of the world (John 8:12), door/gate for the sheep (John 10:7-9), the resurrection and the life (John 11:25), the good shepherd (John 10:11), the way, the truth, and the life (John 14:6), and the true vine (John 15:1-5)

41. Only through Jesus (John 14:6)

42. A donkey (John 12:14)

Questions

43. In communion, what does the bread and wine represent?

44 How long was Jesus in the tomb?

45. How long was Jesus on earth between his resurrection and ascension?

46. After Jesus is resurrected, how many times does He ask Peter if He loves him?

47. Which three languages were written on the notice that Pilate placed on Jesus' cross?

48. What was the significance of the temple veil being town in two?

49. How is Jesus represented in regards to Passover?

50. What does it mean to repent?

51. What was Luke's occupation?

52. What disciple replaced Judas Iscariot after he betrayed Jesus?

the Bible is good for you

Answer Key

43. Jesus' broken body and His blood (Luke 22:19-20)

44. Three days and three nights (Matthew 12:40)

45. 40 days

46. 3 (John 21:15-17)

47. Hebrew, Latin, and Greek (John 19:20)

48. God's presence was no longer contained in one location

49. As the Lamb of God (John 1:29)

50. To acknowledge and turn away from your sins

51. A doctor

52. Matthias (Acts 1:26)

Questions

53. What happens to the disciples and other believers at the beginning of Acts?

54. How many people are added to the church on the day of Pentecost in the book of Acts?

55. Who is stoned to death for their faith in Jesus?

56. Who held the coats of the men stoning Stephen?

57. What was Paul's Jewish name?

58. Who was Paul's rabbi?

59. What city was Paul heading to when he met Jesus?

60. What was the name of Paul's hometown?

61. How long did Paul spend in Tarsus before going on his first missionary journey?

62. Who joined Paul on his first missionary journey?

63. What was the Jerusalem Council?

the Bible is good for you

Answer Key

53. They receive the Holy Spirit (Acts 2:4)

54. 3,000 (Acts 2:41)

55. Stephen (Acts 7:57-58)

56. Paul (Acts 7:58)

57. Saul

58. Gamaliel (Acts 22:3)

59. Damascus (Acts 9:3)

60. Tarsus (Acts 21:39)

61. 14 years

62. Barnabas (Acts 13:3)

63. A meeting to decide if Gentile Christians needed to observe Mosaic Law (Acts 15)

Questions

64. How many missionary journeys did Paul go on?

65. What island was Paul shipwrecked on?

66. Who was in prison with Paul when their chains were loosened after singing worship music?

67. What is an epistle?

68. Who wrote the majority of the New Testament letters?

69. What does Paul say can separate us from the love of God?

70. What does sanctification mean?

71. What chapter in the New Testament is considered the "love chapter"?

72. Which spiritual gift does Paul say we should "eagerly desire"?

73. Where the spirit of the Lord is, there is what?

the Bible is good for you

Answer Key

64. 4 (Acts 13:4-15:35; 15:36-18:22; 18:23-21:17; 27:1-28:16)

65. Malta (Acts 28:1)

66. Silas (Acts 16:25-26)

67. A letter

68. Paul

69. Nothing (Romans 8:38-39)

70. To become holy

71. 1 Corinthians 13

72. Prophecy (1 Corinthians 14:1)

73. Freedom (2 Corinthians 3:17)

Questions

74. How many characteristics does the Fruit of the Holy Spirit contain?

75. What 9 characteristics make up the Fruit of the Holy Spirit?

76. Who was the book of Ephesians written to?

77. In the "armor of God" from Ephesians 6, what does the sword represent?

78. Which part of the "armor of God" is associated with salvation?

79. How does the book of Ephesians say that children can live a long life on Earth?

80. Where did Paul write the book of Philippians from?

81. Which letters from Paul are known as the "Prison Epistles"?

82. How often are believers instructed to pray?

the Bible is good for you

Answer Key

74 9 (Galatians 5:22-23)

75. Love, Joy, Peace, Patience, Kindness, Goodness, Faithfulness, Gentleness, Self-Control (Galatians 5:22-23)

76. The church in Ephesus (Ephesians 1:1)

77. The Sword of the Spirit aka the Bible (Ephesians 6:17)

78. The helmet (Ephesians 6:17)

79. By honoring their parents (Ephesians 6:2)

80. Jail (Philippians 1:13)

81. Ephesians, Philippians, Colossians, Philemon

82. Continually

Questions

83. Which letters from Paul are known as the "Pastoral Epistles"?

84. What role does Paul play in the life of Timothy?

85. Aside from Paul, who was Timothy's other Christian mentor?

86. What is the only letter of recommendation in the Bible?

87. In the book of Philemon, who is Paul asking forgiveness for?

88. The Word of God is sharper than what?

89. What chapter of the Bible is considered the "Hall of Faith"?

90. What five books did John write?

91. According to the book of James, faith without what is dead?

the Bible is good for you

Answer Key

83. 1 and 2 Timothy and Titus

84. His spiritual father (1 Timothy 1:2)

85. Barnabas

86. The book of Philemon

87. Onesimus (Philemon 1:10)

88. Any double-edged sword (Hebrews 4:12)

89. Hebrews 11

90. Gospel of John, 1 John, 2 John, 3 John, and Revelation

91. Works (James 2:17)

Questions

92. What is the purpose of spiritual gifts?

93. What was the last book that Paul wrote before his death?

94. How long will the Kingdom of God last?

95. In the book of Jude, which archangel is said to have argued with the devil over the body of Moses?

96. What is the shortest book of the New Testament?

97. What island did John have the vision of Revelation on?

98. What is the only book of the Bible that says you will be blessed by reading it?

99. What number does John repeat throughout the book of Revelation?

100. According to Revelation, how long will Jesus reign on Earth after His second coming?

the Bible is good for you

Answer Key

92. To serve one another and bring glory to Jesus (1 Peter 4:10-11)

93. Second Timothy

94. Forever (2 Peter 1:11)

95. Michael (Jude 1:9)

96. Jude

97. The Island of Patmos

98. Revelation (Revelation 1:3)

99. 7 (Revelation 1:4, 5:6, 10:3, etc)

100. 1,000 years (Revelation 20:4)

DID YOU KNOW?

The apostle Paul was a tent maker.

The disciple Peter was crucified upside down.

DID YOU KNOW?

The word "amen" means "so be it".

The word "Christian" only appears in the Bible three times. (Acts 11:26, Acts 26:28, 1 Peter 4:16)

Zach Windahl

Zach Windahl has helped thousands of people understand the Bible better and grow closer to God. He runs the brand Sunday and is the author of several books including The Bible Study, The Best Season Planner, and the Sunday Journal. He lives in Miami, Florida.

Conclusion

Sunday Bible Trivia is a book of 200 trivia questions designed to test your knowledge of the Bible, whether you are a new believer or advanced in your faith.

To view our other products, such as, The Bible Study, The Best Season Planner, Sunday Table Talk, and the Sunday journal, visit *www.thebrandsunday.com*.

THE
BIBLE
IS
GOOD
FOR
YOU

SUNDAY.